Sara Swan Miller

Frogs and Toads

The Leggy Leapers

Franklin Watts - A Division of Grolier Publishing
New York • London • Hong Kong • Sydney • Danbury, Connecticut

For Ilka
"Swims-with-the-Frogs"

Photographs ©: Animals Animals: 39 (K. Atkinson/OSF), 18, 19 (M. Fogden/OSF), 33 (Paul Freed), 29 (John Netherton), 25 (Juan Manuel Renjifo); Biofotos: 42 (Brian Rogers); Gallo Images: 31 (Vincent Carruthers); Heather Angel Photo Library: 1, 6, 17, 21, 23; Monkmeyer Press: 7 (Lanks), 5 top left, 5 bottom left (Rue); NHPA: 41 (A.N.T.), 27 (Daniel Heuclin); Photo Researchers: 5 top right (F. Gohier), 35 (Nuridsany et Perennou); Visuals Unlimited: 15 (Bill Beatty), 12, 13 (Joe McDonald), 5 bottom right, 37 (Jim Merli), 43 (Rob & Ann Simpson), cover (William J. Weber).

Illustrations by Jose Gonzales and Steve Savage

The photograph on the cover shows a North American bullfrog. The photo on the title page shows a pickerel frog leaping.

Visit Franklin Watts on the Internet at:
http://publishing.grolier.com

Library of Congress Cataloging-in-Publication Data

Miller, Sara Swan.
Frogs and toads: the leggy leapers / Sara Swan Miller.
    p. cm. — (Animals in order)
    Includes bibliographical references and index.
    Summary: Describes the general characteristics of frogs and toads and takes a close look at fifteen species.
    ISBN 0-531-11632-8 (lib. bdg.)   0-531-16495-0 (pbk.)
    1. Anura—juvenile literature. [1. Frogs. 2. Toads.] I. Title. II. Series.
QL668.E2 M53   2000
597.8 21—dc21
                                                                    99-042710
                                                                    CIP

Contents

Looking at Frogs and Toads

Have you ever heard peepers trilling from a pond in the early spring? Have you seen a bullfrog sitting by the water's edge, waiting for an insect to happen by? Maybe you have watched a toad hopping about in the garden.

You might have suspected that frogs and toads are related. In fact, scientists place them in the same group, or *order*, of animals. That order is called anura. Frogs and toads have certain things in common that other animals don't share.

Look at the two frogs and two toads shown on the next page. Do you know how they are all alike?

North American bullfrog

Darwin's frog

American toad

Fire-bellied toad

Traits of Frogs and Toads

Frogs and toads are *amphibians*. They lay their eggs in water because the eggs don't have shells tough enough to keep them from drying out. When the tadpoles hatch, they live in the water and breathe through gills. Adult frogs and toads live on land and breathe through their skin and their lungs.

Frogs and toads are different from other amphibians. Unlike salamanders, for instance, they have no tail. Frogs and toads do have long, strong legs and extra-long ankle bones that are perfect for leaping or hopping. Many have webbed toes that help them swim swiftly.

Frogs and toads can see the slightest movements. When you walk toward a pond or stream, you'll often hear frogs splashing to safety in the water. If you stay very still, the frogs will soon come out again

Tadpoles look similar to fish.

and sit watchfully on the bank. Frogs and toads also use their big, bulging eyes to find the insects they eat. They can see in every direction, even though their eyes don't move in their sockets. When a frog or toad catches an insect, it pushes its eyes down into the sockets and against the roof of its mouth to help it swallow. The animal looks as if it's blinking.

The ears of frogs and toads are called *tympani*. They are located on the sides of their head. Those ears are especially important during mating time. Only males call for a mate. Each species has a special call, so a female can tell when the right male is calling. The male makes his vocal cords vibrate by forcing air through his larynx, or voice box. Most males have a pouch of skin on their throat called a *vocal sac*. The pouch acts like a loudspeaker.

This American toad is calling for a mate.

What is the difference between a frog and a toad? Usually, frogs are slim and slippery and have long back legs. Toads are usually squat, slow-moving creatures with dry, bumpy skin. But you can't always tell whether an animal is a frog or a toad just from the way it looks. Scientists tell the difference by looking at the way the animals' bones are arranged.

The Order of Living Things

A tiger has more in common with a house cat than with a daisy. A true bug is more like a butterfly than a jellyfish. Scientists arrange living things into groups based on how they look and how they act. A tiger and a house cat belong to the same group, but a daisy belongs to a different group.

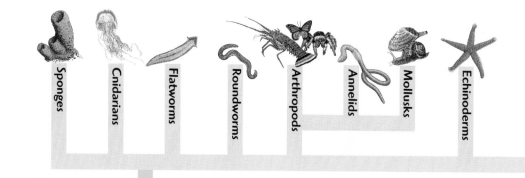

Sponges Cnidarians Flatworms Roundworms Arthropods Annelids Mollusks Echinoderms

Animals

Plants Fungi

Protists

Monerans

All living things can be placed in one of five groups called *kingdoms*: the plant kingdom, the animal kingdom, the fungus kingdom, the moneran kingdom, or the protist kingdom. You can probably name many of the creatures in the plant and animal kingdoms. The fungus kingdom includes mushrooms, yeasts, and molds. The moneran and protist kingdoms contain thousands of living things that are too small to see without a microscope.

8

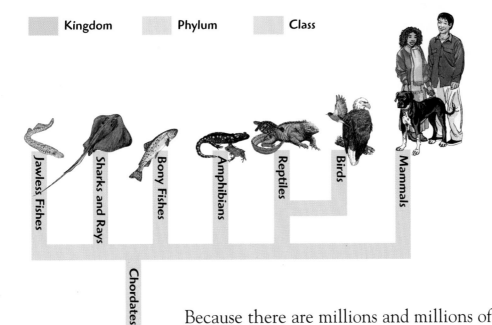

Kingdom Phylum Class

Jawless Fishes

Sharks and Rays

Bony Fishes

Amphibians

Reptiles

Birds

Mammals

Chordates

Because there are millions and millions of living things on Earth, some of the members of one kingdom may not seem all that similar. The animal kingdom includes creatures as different as tarantulas and trout, jellyfish and jaguars, salamanders and sparrows, elephants and earthworms.

To show that an elephant is more like a jaguar than an earthworm, scientists further separate the creatures in each kingdom into more specific groups. The animal kingdom can be divided into nine *phyla*. Humans belong to the chordate phylum. Almost all chordates have a backbone.

Each phylum can be subdivided into many *classes*. Humans, mice, and elephants all belong to the mammal class. Each class can be further divided into orders; orders into *families*, families into *genera*, and genera into *species*. All the members of a species are very similar.

How Frogs and Toads Fit In

You can probably guess that frogs and toads belong to the animal kingdom. They have much more in common with swordfish and snakes than with maple trees and morning glories.

Frogs and toads belong to the chordate phylum. Almost all chordates have a backbone and a skeleton. Can you think of other chordates? Examples include elephants, mice, turtles, salamanders, birds, fish, and whales.

All amphibians belong to the same class. There are three different orders of amphibians. Amphibians are among nature's most interesting creatures. When the young hatch, they breathe through gills, like fish. When they grow up, however, they develop lungs and breathe like other land animals.

Frogs and toads make up one order of amphibians. Salamanders belong to another order. The third kind of amphibian is called a caecilian. Because a caecilian has no legs, it looks like a cross between a snake and an earthworm.

Frogs and toads are divided into a number of different families and genera. These groups are broken down into more than 3,500 species, and they live in all parts of the world—even in deserts and very cold places. Each species has its own call, different ways of surviving and protecting its young, and a special place in its environment. In this book, you will learn more about fifteen species of frogs and toads.

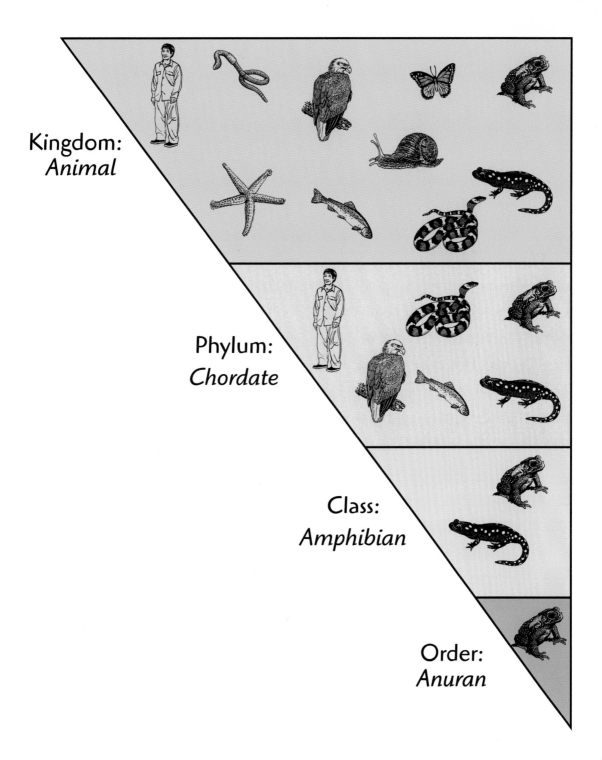

Kingdom:
Animal

Phylum:
Chordate

Class:
Amphibian

Order:
Anuran

True Frogs

FAMILY: Ranidae
COMMON EXAMPLE: North American bullfrog
GENUS AND SPECIES: *Rana catesbeiana*
Size: 3 1/2 to 8 inches (9 to 20 cm)

"JUG O' RUM. JUG O' RUM." A big male bullfrog sits at the edge of a pond, calling loudly for his mate. You can hear him from more than 1,000 feet (305 meters) away. A female hears him, too. She swims up to find him. The male climbs on her back, hugging her with his front legs. She carries him about as she swims along. Finally, she lays a mass of eggs, and he covers them with *sperm* to *fertilize* them.

When the tadpoles hatch, they grow gills on the sides of their heads. They swim about, scraping tiny bits of food from water plants. For 2 or 3 years, the tadpoles grow bigger and bigger. Finally, they grow back legs. Then front legs appear. The tadpoles' mouths grow wider, and they develop lungs. Slowly, they absorb their tails. At last they're ready to leap about on land.

Like other frogs and toads, a bullfrog is a *predator*. It sits on a bank and waits for its *prey*. It eats mostly insects, crayfish, minnows, and other frogs. A big bull-

12

frog can catch and swallow birds and snakes. Some have even been seen catching bats.

Bullfrogs have lots of enemies, too, from herons to snakes to raccoons. Even though a female may lay up to 20,000 eggs at a time, only about 200 will survive to have tadpoles of their own.

True Toads

FAMILY: Bufonidae
COMMON EXAMPLE: American toad
GENUS AND SPECIES: *Bufo americanus*
Size: 2 to 3 1/2 inches (5 to 9 cm)

A toad squats quietly under a plant. It looks as though it's taking a nap. When a beetle crawls by, the toad's long, sticky tongue flashes out and grabs the prey. The toad blinks as it swallows its meal.

Like other true toads, the American toad moves slowly. It has a wide body and shorter legs than a frog. When it moves from its hiding place, the toad walks or hops instead of leaping like a frog.

A toad doesn't have to move fast to escape its enemies. It has other ways to defend itself. Its colors blend in with its surroundings, so most other animals don't see it. Its bumpy skin has *glands* that give off a milky, poisonous fluid, so most predators avoid it. The American toad has another trick, too. If a snake comes hunting, the toad puffs itself up until it looks much too big to swallow.

Like other amphibians, toads can't stand too much heat or cold. In the heat of a summer day, they rest in the shade. When cold weather comes, they dig themselves backward into the soft ground and *hibernate*, or rest, for the winter.

In the spring, you can hear males calling for mates, trilling a pleasant "bu-rr-r-r-r." Soon after, you may find long strings of toad eggs stuck on water plants.

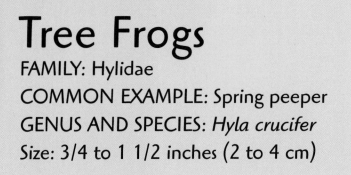

Tree Frogs

FAMILY: Hylidae
COMMON EXAMPLE: Spring peeper
GENUS AND SPECIES: *Hyla crucifer*
Size: 3/4 to 1 1/2 inches (2 to 4 cm)

Have you ever heard a high, sweet sound like the jingling of bells coming from a pond in the early spring? You were listening to a chorus of male spring peepers. They are one of the first signs of spring.

Peepers spend most of their time in bushes and grasses near the water. The sticky pads on their feet help them hold on. A peeper can even climb up a pane of glass.

Peepers wait motionless for insects to come by, and then snatch their prey with their long, sticky tongues. Like other frogs and toads, the peeper's tongue is attached to the front part of its mouth and it flips out in an instant.

Peepers have a lot of enemies, including snakes, birds, and owls. Luckily, their spotty, brown color blends right in with the branches they cling to.

In the spring, male peepers call from bushes hanging over the water, and soon the females come out of the woods to find them. A male climbs on top of the female and hugs his mate tightly. She carries him to a nearby pond and lays her eggs. The tiny tadpoles grow fast. By winter, they are fully grown and ready to hibernate until spring.

Rhinoderma Frogs

FAMILY: Rhinodermatidae
COMMON EXAMPLE: Darwin's frog
GENUS AND SPECIES: *Rhinoderma darwinii*
SIZE: 1 1/4 inches (3 cm)

The Darwin's frog has a very unusual way of protecting its young. To begin with, a female lays her eggs on land. The male then sits beside the eggs until they are ready to hatch. When he sees the tadpoles wiggling inside the eggs, the male scoops them up in his mouth.

The tadpoles don't go down into their father's stomach, though. They go into the long vocal sacs that run down the sides of his body. Safe inside, the tadpoles slowly develop into frogs.

What do they eat in there? Each tadpole has a supply of yolk from its egg that keeps it well fed. After 2 or 3 months, the tadpoles turn into frogs. When the young frogs are fully developed, their father opens his mouth, and a dozen tiny frogs come hopping out.

Darwin's frog has a close relative that also lays its eggs on land. Like Darwin's frog, the male takes the eggs into his mouth when they're ready to hatch. But then he carries them down to the water and lets them go. Those tiny tadpoles have to fend for themselves.

Both kinds of frogs live in the cool forests of Chile and Argentina. Darwin's frogs are named after Charles Darwin, the famous naturalist who discovered them. Imagine his surprise when he saw tiny frogs hopping out of a big frog's mouth.

Marsupial Frogs

FAMILY: Hylidae
COMMON EXAMPLE: Marsupial tree frog
GENUS AND SPECIES: *Gastrotheca marsupiata*
SIZE: 2 1/2 inches (6 cm)

The marsupial tree frog lives in South America. It has a special way of protecting its young. Like a female kangaroo, a female marsupial frog has a pouch. A kangaroo's pouch is on its belly, but a marsupial tree frog's pouch is on its back. A marsupial frog's pouch is made of thin skin, and you can see the eggs inside.

At mating time, the male stays with the female as she lays her eggs. He fertilizes them and then pushes them into her pouch with his feet.

The female lays a lot of eggs at one time, so she looks very lumpy and swollen just before they hatch. When the tadpoles are ready, their mother helps them come out. She pulls apart the slit-like opening of the pouch with one of her back toes. Then the tiny tadpoles escape and make their own way in the world.

A close relative of the marsupial tree frog also carries its eggs on its back, but it doesn't have a pouch. The eggs just stick there, unprotected. If an enemy comes near, the mother quickly leaps away with her precious cargo.

Pipoid Frogs

FAMILY: Pipidae
COMMON EXAMPLE: Surinam toad
GENUS AND SPECIES: *Pipa pipa*
SIZE: 8 inches (20 cm)

The Surinam toad is one of the strangest toads in the world. It looks like a flat, square pancake with a leg on each corner.

This South American toad spends almost all its time in the water, hunting for worms, insects, and small fish. Its back feet are webbed, but its front feet are not. Each of the three toes on its front feet ends in a star-shaped organ that helps the toad find food.

A Surinam toad has no tongue. It uses its sensitive front toes to probe for food on the muddy bottom. When it finds prey, it stuffs the food into its mouth with its front feet. This toad has no vocal cords either, but the male can make a clicking sound with bony rods inside his throat.

One of the most curious things about a Surinam toad is the way the female protects her eggs. As she lays her eggs, the male fertilizes them, and they fall onto the female's back. Then skin grows over them, forming a kind of a bubble with a horny lid. She may have as many as 100 eggs on her back.

The female carries the eggs for about 5 months. During this time, the tadpoles hatch and become toads. Finally, dozens of tiny, fully formed toads pop out of the bubble on her back and swim away.

Poison Frogs

FAMILY: Dendrobatidae

COMMON EXAMPLE: Golden poison frog

GENUS AND SPECIES: *Phyllobates terribilis*

SIZE: 1/2 to 2 inches (1 to 5 cm)

The golden poison frog may be small, but it is deadly. Its bright yellow color is a warning that other creatures had better pay attention to: "Don't touch me!" One frog's skin has enough poison to kill 100 people.

Some native people in South America discovered how deadly this frog is, and have found a way to use its poison. They heat the tips of their blowgun darts and wipe them over a poison frog's back to make a deadly weapon for hunting small prey. The blowgun dart stays poisonous for more than 1 year.

A golden poison frog spends most of its time in trees. The tiny, sticky disks on its toes help the frog cling to slippery leaves and tree trunks. When a small insect comes by, out zips a long, sticky tongue. The insect vanishes in a flash.

At breeding time, a female lays her eggs in the moist leaves on the forest floor and leaps away. The male guards the eggs and keeps them moist. Finally, when the eggs are ready to hatch, the male frees the tadpoles from the jellylike mass with his back legs. They wiggle onto his back, and he carries them to a stream where they can swim free.

Ranids

FAMILY: Ranidae
COMMON EXAMPLE: Goliath frog
GENUS AND SPECIES: *Conraua goliath*
SIZE: 12 inches (30 cm)

It's easy to see how the Goliath frog got its name—it's a giant. In fact, it's the biggest frog in the world. Its body is 12 inches (30 cm) long, and with its legs stretched out, it measures more than 30 inches (76 cm). This huge frog is heavy, too. It weighs as much as a large housecat.

Believe it or not, the world's largest frogs cannot make even the tiniest sound. They have no vocal sacs. Like most other frogs, though, they do have slippery skin covered with a slimy substance called *mucus*. Mucus helps keep their skin moist.

On land, these giant, long-legged frogs are powerful jumpers. In the water, where they spend most of their time, their long legs and big webbed feet make them strong swimmers.

The females lay their eggs in clumps in the water and swim away. You might think that these giant frogs would have giant tadpoles, but their young are the same size as any other tadpoles.

Goliath frogs live in deep rivers in the rain forests of West Africa. When droughts come and the streams are low, the native people often catch these frogs for food. After a meal, they dry the prized leg bones and use them to predict the future.

Reed Frogs

FAMILY: Hyperoliidae
COMMON EXAMPLE: Pygmy leaf-folding frog
GENUS AND SPECIES: *Afrixalus pygmaeus*
SIZE: 3/4 inch (2 cm)

It is the middle of the African rainy season, and that means it is mating time for pygmy leaf-folding frogs. All night long, the air is alive with the buzzing sound of males calling for their mates. For weeks and weeks, the males keep calling. They don't stop when they find a female and mate. Their goal is to mate with as many females as possible.

It's easy to find these frogs at night, but if you tried to find one during the day, you would probably have a hard time. These tiny frogs are no bigger than your thumb. During the day, they hide in the reeds that grow along the shores of ponds and marshes. Their light-brown bodies mottled with darker brown help them blend in with their surroundings.

Can you guess how the pygmy leaf-folding frog got its name? The female lays her eggs on a leaf, folds the leaf around them, and then seals the edges of the leaf with a liquid produced by her body. Inside the leaf, the eggs are safe until they are ready to hatch.

Ghost Frogs

FAMILY: Heleophrinidae
COMMON EXAMPLE: Cape ghost frog
GENUS AND SPECIES: *Heleophryne purcelli*
SIZE: 1 to 2 1/2 inches (2.5 to 6.5 cm)

How did this little frog get its name? It doesn't look ghostly, and it certainly doesn't leap out from its hiding place and say "Boo!" It's called the ghost frog because one kind lives in a place called Skeleton Gorge.

Ghost frogs live only in the southernmost part of Africa. They are well suited to life in and around the fast-flowing mountain streams that run through their *habitats*. The adults are flatter than most frogs, so they can hide in cracks at the sides of streams. Their large, sticky toes help them cling to slippery rocks in a stream or along the water's edge.

The females lay their eggs in the water. They stick the egg masses to underwater plants, sticks, or stones to keep them from being swept downstream.

Like other tadpoles that live in fast-flowing streams, young ghost frogs have large sucking disks for mouths. They latch onto slippery rocks or underwater sticks so that they can stay in one spot to feed.

The tadpoles use rows of tiny, tooth-like points in their mouth to scrape *algae* from stones and sticks to feed on. Within a few weeks, the tadpoles change into wide-mouthed, insect-eating adults.

Foam-Nest Tree Frogs

FAMILY: Rhacophoridae

COMMON EXAMPLE: Gray tree frog

GENUS AND SPECIES: *Chiromantis*
  xerampelina

SIZE: 2 to 2 1/2 inches (5 to 6 cm)

Most frogs lay their eggs in the water, but gray tree frogs lay their eggs in trees. How do they keep the eggs from drying out? They protect them with a nest of foam.

When a male and a female find each other, they look for a nesting spot in a tree overhanging the water. The male clings to the female's back while she releases some liquid from an opening on her back end. The two frogs beat the liquid with their back feet until it's foamy—like egg whites beaten with an eggbeater.

The female lays her eggs in the foam and adds more liquid. The frogs keep beating until the foamy nest is about 8 inches (20 cm) across. After about 3 hours, the nest is ready. The female jumps down into the pond to rest, and the male hops off to mate again.

The frothy foam nest dries on the outside and turns crusty and brown. The eggs inside stay moist until the tadpoles begin to hatch about a week later. The young swim about inside the nest for a few days. All that movement warms the nest, causing it to soften and break apart. Then, one by one, the tadpoles drop into the pond below.

32

Midwife Toads

FAMILY: Discoglossidae
COMMON EXAMPLE: Midwife toad
GENUS AND SPECIES: *Alytes obstetricans*
SIZE: 1 to 3 inches (2.5 to 8 cm)

The midwife toad is another amphibian with a special way of protecting its eggs from enemies. In this case, though, the male does the work.

While a female is laying her eggs on land, the male pushes his back legs through the long double string of eggs until it is wrapped around his body. When the female has finished laying her eggs, she hops away. The male hides in a *burrow*—wearing the eggs like an odd piece of jewelry—until night falls.

When it is dark, the male comes out to hunt for food. As he hops about, dew on the ground moistens the eggs. On dry nights, the male keeps the eggs moist by diving into the water with them.

When the male senses that the eggs are ready to hatch, he heads for the nearest pool of water. The tadpoles hatch in the water and swim off. They grow slowly. At least a year passes before the little toads hop out onto land.

You probably won't see midwife toads during the day. They hide in their burrows, where they are safe from the hot sun. At night, they come out to hunt. Then, at dawn, they always return to the same cool burrow.

Midwife toads live in many different habitats—from sand dunes to mountains. They are even found on high mountain peaks, where the ground is frozen most of the year.

Fire-Bellied Toads

FAMILY: Bombinatoridae
COMMON EXAMPLE: Oriental fire-bellied
    toad
GENUS AND SPECIES: *Bombina orientalis*
SIZE: 2 to 3 inches (5 to 8 cm)

A fire-bellied toad floats quietly among the water lilies, looking like any other dull-gray toad. A heron stalking through the marsh soon spots the toad. The bird rears up to strike, but the toad is ready. Suddenly, it throws its head back, arches its back, raises its legs, and flashes its bright, red-orange belly.

The startled heron backs off. The bird stalks away, looking for something else to eat, and the toad settles down in the lilies.

A fire-bellied toad can do more than just startle a predator. That fire-colored belly is a warning. The toad's skin contains a poison that can burn the mouth of any creature that tries to eat it.

In the spring and summer, the males call for their mates with a honking, barking sound. The females lay only about a hundred eggs at a time, but they lay several sets. Each egg sticks to a water plant or a stick.

When the tadpoles hatch, they are dull-colored. Their bellies don't develop their bright colors until about a year after the toads come onto land.

Burrowing Tree Frogs

FAMILY: Hylidae
COMMON EXAMPLE: Water-holding frog
GENUS AND SPECIES: *Cyclorana platycephala*
SIZE: 1 1/2 to 3 inches (4 to 8 cm)

The water-holding frog is a tree frog, but it doesn't live in trees. It spends most of its life in a burrow underground. It stores water in its bladder or in pouches under its skin.

This frog lives in the deserts of southern Australia. For most of the year, the ground is too hot and dry for a frog to be out and about. The only way to escape the desert heat is to burrow into the ground and wait for the rainy season.

The frog uses skin sheddings and mucus to line the walls of its burrow. When this lining hardens, it forms an extra outer "skin" that keeps the frog from drying out. Surrounded by its special "skin," the frog sleeps the weeks away.

When the rains come at last, the frog tears open its burrow and comes out to mate. Females lay their eggs in a shallow pool. The water may be very warm—too warm for any other tadpoles—but water-holding tadpoles can stand the heat.

The pool will soon dry up in the hot sun, so the tadpoles have only a very short time to develop into adult frogs. Then they will dig themselves into the ground and wait for the rains to come again.

Desert travelers who know how to find these frogs sometimes use them as a source of water. If you gently squeeze a water-holding frog, it will release its supply of fresh water. This does not harm the frog.

Gastric Brooding Frogs

FAMILY: Myobatrachidae
COMMON NAME: Gastric brooding frog
GENUS AND SPECIES: *Rheobatrachus silus*
SIZE: 2 inches (5 cm)

Many frogs and toads have strange ways of protecting their eggs and young. The gastric brooding frog may have the strangest way of all.

After the female lays her eggs, the male fertilizes them. Then the female swallows them, and the young develop in her stomach.

Why doesn't the female digest the eggs? The eggs—and later the tadpoles—are surrounded by a jellylike material. This jelly contains chemicals that shut down the mother's digestive juices. She doesn't eat for 6 long weeks, until the young frogs come hopping out of her mouth.

Scientists discovered the gastric brooding frog in 1973. Before then, scientists didn't think any water-living frogs lived in Australia. Gastric brooding frogs are shy creatures. They spend most of their time hiding under stones on the bottom of ponds. That is probably why it took so long to find them.

Scientists were excited when they discovered that young gastric brooders live in their mother's stomach. They hoped that by studying these frogs, they might be able to develop a medicine to help people with stomach ulcers.

Sadly, gastric brooding frogs haven't been seen in their natural
habitat for many years. Many scientists think that they may have
all died.

Will Frogs and Toads Disappear?

Frogs and toads are among the oldest groups of animals on Earth. They have lived on our planet for millions and millions of years. In recent years, scientists have begun to realize that many species of frogs and toads are disappearing.

There are many reasons that these amphibians are dying out. As rain forests are cut for timber or cleared for farming, some of the places frogs and toads live are destroyed. As swamps and marshes are drained and turned into farmland or building sites, other frogs and toads lose their homes.

This area of rain forest has been destroyed so farmers can plant crops.

There are other dangers, too. Frogs and toads absorb pollution from the air, soil, and water through their moist skins. The chemicals that farmers spray on their crops poison frogs and toads. In many parts of the world, people pour oil and other chemicals on ponds to kill mosquitoes. The frogs and toads living in those ponds die too.

When acid rain falls on the lakes and ponds, frogs and toads are the first animals to feel the effects. Even a slight change in the amount of acid in the water can kill eggs and tadpoles. As cars and factories pump carbon dioxide into the air, Earth's climate seems to be changing. There are more droughts in some areas and more floods in other places. When an area gets less rain, ponds dry up and the amphibians that live in them die.

Fortunately, many people are worried about frogs and toads. They are trying to save amphibian habitats and decrease pollution. There is still hope that frogs and toads will survive for many more millions of years.

When frog eggs come into contact with chemicals, the animals that grow from them may have extra body parts. This frog has six legs.

43

Words to Know

algae—a tiny plant-like creature that serves as food for many species of tadpoles

amphibian—an animal that lives in the water when it is young, and moves onto land as an adult

burrow—a shelter dug in the ground

class—a group of animals within a phylum that share certain characteristics

family—a group of creatures within an order that share certain characteristics

fertilize—to mix eggs and sperm to create a new individual

genus (plural **genera**)—a group of creatures within a family that share certain characteristics

gland—an organ in an animal's body that secretes fluids, such as mucus and poisons

habitat—the place where a plant or an animal spends its life

hibernate—to spend the winter in a resting, inactive state

kingdom—one of the five divisions into which all living things are placed: the animal kingdom, the plant kingdom, the fungus kingdom, the moneran kingdom, and the protist kingdom

mucus—a slippery fluid secreted by mucous membranes

order—a group of creatures within a class that share certain characteristics

phylum (plural **phyla**)—a group of creatures within a kingdom that share certain characteristics

predator—an animal that hunts other animals for food

prey—an animal that becomes food for other animals

species—a group of creatures within a genus that share certain characteristics. Members of a species can mate and produce young.

sperm—reproductive cells produced and released by male animals

tympanum (plural **tympani**)—a drumlike membrane on the side of a frog or toad's head that allows it to hear

vocal sac—an air sac that makes a frog or toad's call louder

Learning More

Books

Martin, James, and Art Wolfe. *Frogs*. New York: Crown Publishing, 1997.

Pascoe, Elaine, Dwight Kuhn, and Nicole Bowman (editor). *Tadpoles*. Woodbridge, CT: Blackbirch Press, 1996.

Quinn, John R., Mara P. William, and Kathy Tucker (editor). *The Fragile Frog*. Chicago: Albert Whitman & Company, 1996.

Web Sites

The Froggy Page
http://frog.simplenet.com/froggy/sciam/shtml
This site features pictures, sounds, games, clip art, links, and more.

Frogland
http://allaboutfrogs.org
Look here for the frog of the month, interesting trivia about frogs and toads, myths and legends about amphibians, book lists, and many links to other sites.

A Thousand Friends of Frogs
http://cgee.hamline.edu/frogs/index.htm
This site offers clear explanations of frog and toad anatomy and life cycles, features student writing and art, and provides information about getting involved in projects to help preserve frogs and toads and their habitats.

Index

About the Author

Sara Swan Miller has enjoyed working with children all her life, first as a nursery-school teacher, and later as an outdoor environmental educator at the Mohonk Preserve in New Paltz, New York. As the director of the Preserve school program, she has led hundreds of children on field trips and taught them the importance of appreciating and respecting the natural world.

She has written a number of children's books, including *Three Stories You Can Read to Your Dog; Three Stories You Can Read to Your Cat; What's in the Woods? An Outdoor Activity Book; Oh, Cats of Camp Rabbitbone!; Piggy in the Parlor and Other Tales; Better Than TV;* and *Will You Sting Me? Will You Bite? The Truth About Some Scary-Looking Insects.* She has also written many other books for the Animals in Order series as well as several books about farm animals for the Children's Press True Books series.